Lost and Found

Shubhangi Daga

BookLeaf
Publishing

India | USA | UK

Presentation by *BookLeaf Publishing*

Web: www.bookleafpub.com

E-mail: info@bookleafpub.com

ISBN: 9789363317321

First edition 2024

ACKNOWLEDGEMENT

The world becomes a better place when you are surrounded by people who encourage you to grow. Friends who make you feel that you must live every moment to the fullest by doing the things they love are the most important people to have. I feel blessed and grateful to have those special few. I would like to thank my friends and family who encouraged me to pursue my endeavors and publish my book. Without all their support and encouragement, this book would not exist.

I would also like to thank my readers. If my poems have taken you down memory lanes, brought a smile to your face, instilled hope, or inspired you, then my purpose is fulfilled. I am truly happy to present this book to you. I hope you enjoy it as much as I enjoyed writing it.

PREFACE

The experiences described in the poems and the
emotions felt while writing each one are
authentic and stem from the author's personal
life experiences. This book is a work of passion,
self-expression, and inspiration. It addresses
feelings that one commonly experiences when
their heart flutters and there is a desire for a
beautiful companionship. It explores finding a
home in another person while not losing sight of
oneself in situations often disguised as love.

~ Artwork by Pavsarts ~

TABLE OF CONTENTS

Straddling in Love

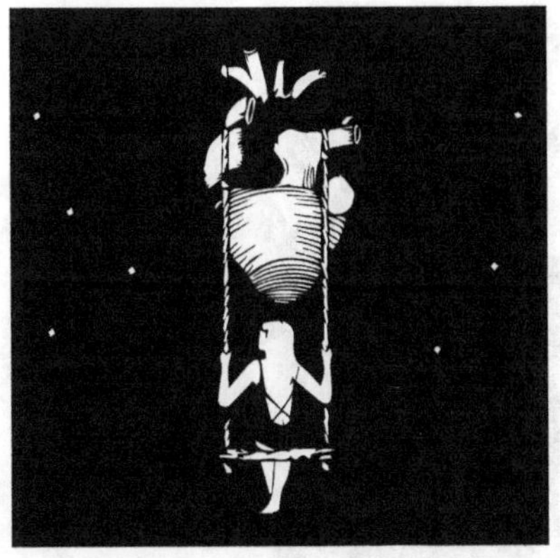

How do we fare
Straddling to be there
In and out of this,
This sweet little affair
You signalled me to beware
With the actions that you flare
I caught you bare
As I became aware
There was nothing left for us to repair

Open or Close

At first your soft knocks at my door
Had me in a frenzy
But then I told myself
Doors are not meant to be held
For those who don't know
Where to stand

Charades

Our love was a game of charades
You always won a point
In my chances to act
But when you acted
I always lost
Until the final time
When I guessed your act
I won the game and
You lost me forever

Inspiration

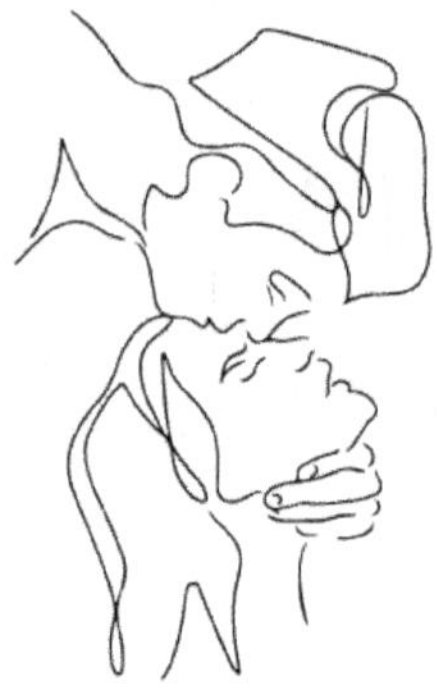

Your words inspire
The growth we aspire
Together we make our lives worthwhile
A life we admire
With greatness that we pile
Happiness that lights up like the flames of fire

Classic Romance

You got me undone
Now I am on the run
As you spilled your magic
You cleared the traffic
You are the one
That adds to the fun
In love with your tactic
We are such a classic

Love Thyself

The times you have lost yourself in love
Remind yourself before anything above
Don't fall for the barbarity
As you are your own priority
For the way you live your dreams
Is way above any worldly schemes
Your life will unleash
The joy like a breeze
Write your adventures, fill a bookshelf
O darling, love thyself!

Eternal Love

Listen to your gut
For it is a must
Listen to what it says
For you may sway
But it may preserve
Ask you to reserve
Your precious heart
That can't be found in a mart
For the dreams you explore
You must always soar
A companion will come along
And tell you where you belong
Witness moments of bliss
In an eternal love such as this

Band-Aid

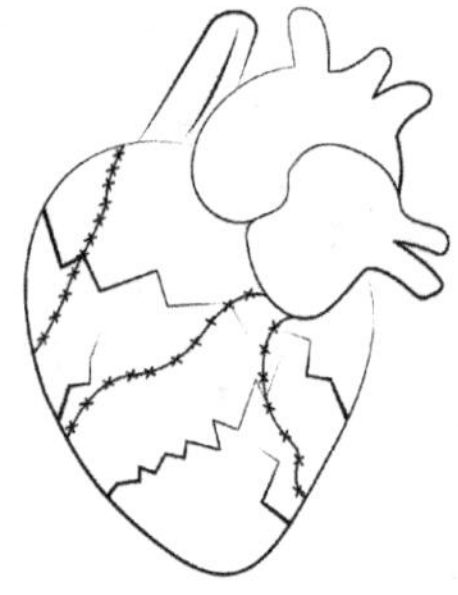

People get played
For the feelings they display
Mending cracks with band-aids
But as time fades
We are left amazed
In ways
A person finally solves the maze

Cupid

The nights we sipped wine
Went out to dine
The nights we talked about life
Went out for drives
Those nights were beautiful
And the memories we created
Words we never spoke
But our hearts played cupid

Waltz

Twirling in the thoughts of you
Swirling in the passion for you
Unfurling this compassion
Whirling in these feelings for you
Emerging to support you
Merging our lives like we are on a mission

Body, Mind and Soul

With my eyes closed
I am waking up
Stepping deeper into my mind
That was clouded with insecurities

With an active body
I am calming down
Cleansing my soul
Filling myself with positivity

With an alert mind
I am letting go
Opening up my chained heart
That was guarded and closed

Purifying my body, mind and soul
I am becoming whole

Longing

Bare body
Naked soul
Longing for the touch
To love me as a whole
It's been a long haul
Since the love in galore
Burning with desire
Are my body and my soul

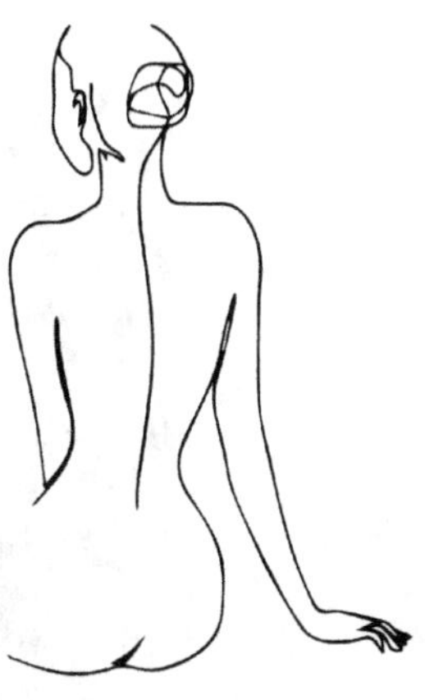

Sunlight

Today, I sit on the beach enthralled by the beauty
of what I see
I look at the sun and admire it for its consistency
It shines bright but not just for me
It shows the light that even you can see

A Patch Up

My broken pieces
Came together
When I stopped picking it up
With my bare hands
And giving it away
To those
Who were gloved

Rising in Love

The sun that rises every day
Waves that form every second
There is hope every day
For the hearts that beat every second
To be happy and sound
Our hearts will sing along
To the tunes of joy with someone, we didn't
know all along
Rising in love unfailing as the sun

Stronger Than Ever

My broken heart became stronger
Through the men who deceived
One after another
It made me ponder
About the love I received
But my heart still grieved
Those who didn't understand
They never stood a chance
I built a shield
To not let myself yield
For those who couldn't love
Had their emotions shoved
But here I am
Stronger than ever
Ready for my one true love

Symphony

We created a symphony that,
our eyes wrote,
our lips sang,
And our hearts felt,
as we danced

En route

A territory unexplored
With emotions that were overboard
This world that we explored
Put us on top of each other's billboard
Our seatbelts are fastened, we're now onboard
The best ride of our lives on this beautiful road

Old School Romance

Let's go back to singing songs to someone
Let's go back to writing letters to someone

Love is a way of expression not suppression

Let's go back to feeling butterflies in the
stomach
Let's go back to feeling dumbstruck

Love is to feel that chuckle
It should make you want to unbuckle

Garden of joy

The joy you feel now
Is what you should vow
To feel every moment, no matter how
You will reap what you sow
Living every moment you will grow
As you water your dreams you always live for

Soulmate

It's the way you are
You light up my path brighter than a shooting
star
The way you care
The bond we share
It's the way you are
We have come so far
You brought in a breath of fresh air
Look at our lives flare
You are an answer to my prayer

Monsoon

The raindrops were set to pour
The wind will add to the galore
The trees and plants will romance more
The earth, spilling a fragrance that's pure
As our eyes locked and brought about the decor
We slow-danced in the rain and went on a tour

Seasons

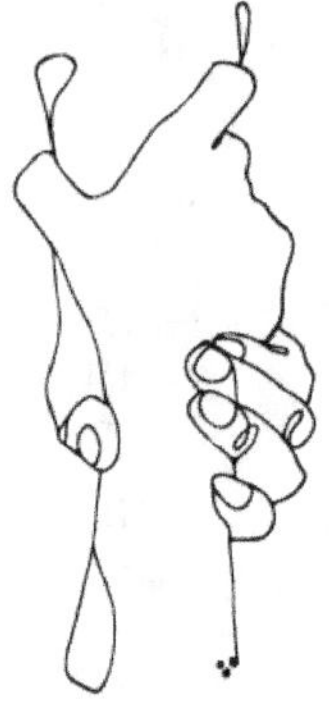

You brought Spring into my life
And transformed my Winter
Into a Summer that was blissful
But Monsoon that was painful
Autumn made us brave
We found each other in all the seasons
And became stronger than ever to brave any
Winter

Date Night

You wore that green shirt I like
I wore black
We're ready to ride
To our special date night
Where there is sweet banter and playful antics
Our forks rolling the spaghetti
Followed by a sip of wine
As the clock ticked nine
The music was fine
Your hand was in mine
You spun me around
Every date night we shined
I am so happy you are mine
As we age like fine wine
Till the time we are fifty-nine
We would still love these date nights
Together having spaghetti and wine

Music Album

Standing close to each other, lost in the music
Tuned into each other's words as if they're
melody
Moving slowly to the sound of the tune
Grooving to the tempo
We realized our hearts sang a symphony
Stronger than the beats of techno
We found harmony in each other's rhythm

Smoothie

Seeing each other after a while
Brought in the freshness of fruits
Your orange-like uniqueness attracted me
Our talk brought in the juiciness of strawberry
We found peace in each other as our lives
churned
With cold milk
A flavourful smoothie that we both made
Tastes the best in the world

Coffee Tasting

You filled the cafe with your aroma
As I saw you walking in
Mesmerized by the sight of you
I spilled a little cappuccino while stirring
You liked a strong flavor as I heard you order an
Americano
You sat across the table from me
You looked at me as I looked at you
Sipping on our coffee, understanding its body
We held hands as we enjoyed the aftertaste of
our fine blends

Grocery Run

Going through the racks of fruits
Is the first time our eyes locked
You seemed like someone I would meet in a
sweet shop
We met another time buying bread at the same
shop
We smiled at each other
and introduced ourselves
A year later
We shared our vows at the altar
Filled with the colors of the vegetables is our
lives
Never running out of spices
We now do grocery runs together

Cloudburst

As the clouds weep today
I sit here in front of you
Nowhere to go
And too far from you
I thought this was it
Until you told me that it's not
Our lives are too different
For it can't be how we had once thought

What if

When I found you, it felt too good to be true
Your actions were supportive
That made me dream of a life that's sorted
I hope it isn't suggestive of something
manipulative
With you by my side, our wins will be reported
I only wish that if it's right, it'll all be positive

Victory

Struggling to steer your life towards victory
It's the fear that consumes you and produces
misery
Unable to stir courage in your life
Our goals and actions nose dive
The wear and tear is natural
But the effort to overcome must be admirable
For there is a choice to rise above
And boldly come out of our cove

Dinner at Nine

Your language is attractive
Your gestures are fine
How can someone be so perfect, I wonder
Screaming around to tell everyone you're mine
The person that you are is so well-defined
You touch hearts with so much ease
It's lovely to see your sharpness like a pine
It's simple to fall in love with you
When I panicked at nine
You were there for me in no time
I love your compassion as we dine
Tiramisu for desserts tasted divine

Playlist switch

Our lives that were playing romantic melodies
Now have a sudden queue of sad songs
A moment in love to another in disillusion
Life suddenly paused the button to happiness
As I regain the power to press play again
I am stronger now to write my own melodies of
joy

Tiptoe

You proposed to me like you meant every word
In no time we were swinging in the air that was
full of love
As reality queued up
We got down from the swing
and tiptoed into life
Where an incognito window closed
And our screens froze

Long Distance Love

You thought about the pros and cons
When you chose me to be the one
When time passes we'll either drift apart or be
one
Our relationship will be put to test
When you're miles away in the West
Your absence is what I miss the most
Waiting for us to meet next is what I dream of

Discarded muffler

You had me around you like a muffler
One that's warm, something you'd never want to
take off
Until a day came when you dropped it
And never came back to pick it up again

Poof

One moment, we were laughing at spoofs
The next, we enjoyed the breeze and stood on
the sunroof
I mistook your plans as being fullproof
As we were going along suddenly, poof
I realized that I am such a goof!

For The Better

It takes two to tango
But when one person doesn't want it
There's nothing that the other can do
I lived in a dream with you in it
To realise some dreams never come true

Final Shot

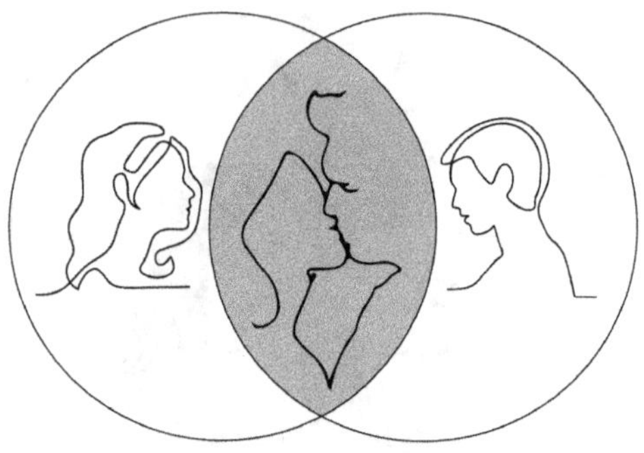

Let's not lie to ourselves about what we feel
today
Let's not speak the words we don't mean
Let's not run away from the reality that we want
A world that you talked to me about
With me in it, is what I want, too
For you are worth fighting for
And I know you want this too

An Ode To You

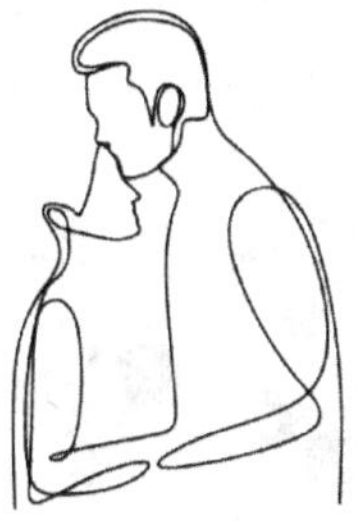

A man as gentle as you
Tall with incredible love to give
I write an ode to how beautiful you are
A person who is large-hearted
I am grateful to have known you

A man as caring as you
Innocent eyes with incredible warmth
I write an ode to how beautiful you are
A person with so much depth
I will always be grateful to have known you

Summer Break

You gave me a summer full of love
I count my blessings that will always have you
on top
You gave me incredible memories
When I reminisce about each one, time freezes
You made me laugh so hard
I recall the moments and wish you didn't play
the wildcard

Telepathy

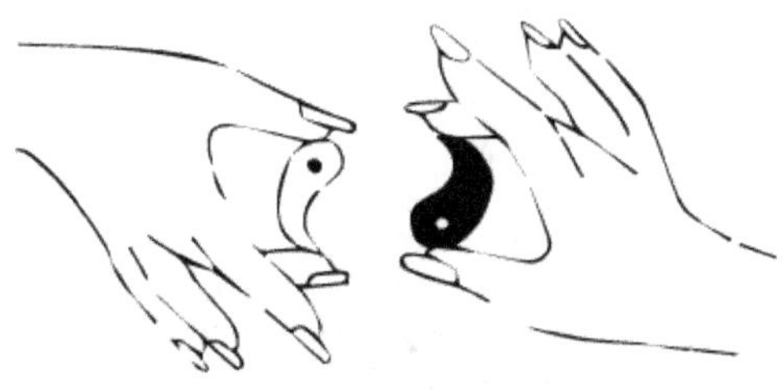

The connection we drew
Was a special one as there are few
A person like you who knew
What was on my mind
And I knew
Your thoughts like I could read you
You spoke what I thought
I read your mind and felt oh my god!
How can this be?
Our rhythm feels free
Expressing what we feel
This telepathic connection with you heals

Bitter Sweet Adieu

I can't stop thinking about you
I'm immersed in your thoughts like never before
I picture how you sat in front of me the last time
we bid adieu
Your eyes spoke about how you didn't want me
to go
As I look outside my window
With wet eyes, I remember you
With only love and gratitude for you

Destiny

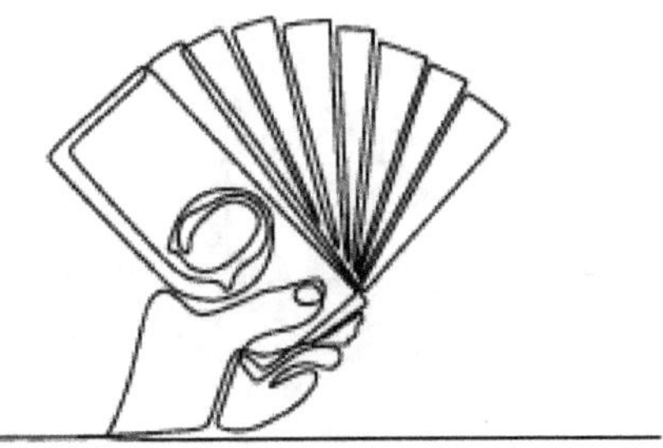

We hold on to each other and take it slow
I hope that our feelings grow
I know that I love you so
If we're truly meant to be we'll glow
Life is a gamble as we know
Stakes are high and sometimes low
Hope we figure it out and not let it blow

Home

Build yourself up with bricks
Coat yourself with concrete
For there can be cracks
In any relationship
Remember the foundation needs to be strong
For any home to stand up firm
There will be ups and downs
But only if you're together you'll rebuild a home

Ups and downs

A little high, a little low
You were like my halo
A little fast, a little slow
You went away in a go

Colors at Dusk

Cotton candy sky
Turned the mood so high
As we sit by the ocean sipping our Mai-tai
Watching the pretty hues in the sky
You took my hand and we ran towards the tide
As we stood in the water you closed my eyes
Feeling an adrenaline high
Sealed with a kiss we bid the sun goodbye

Teamwork

In this journey of life we'll pass through various
thunders
With your arms across my shoulders
Together we'll toss those boulders
We'll be safe despite many roller coasters
As we're equal stakeholders
We'll forever be each other's shareholders

Life's Screenplay

Returning home after a hectic day
I forget about the troubles as I see your face
As we gear up for the next day
You hug me tight in the hallway
It's this moment that I want to replay
We keep doing our best in life's screenplay

Lost in the Abyss

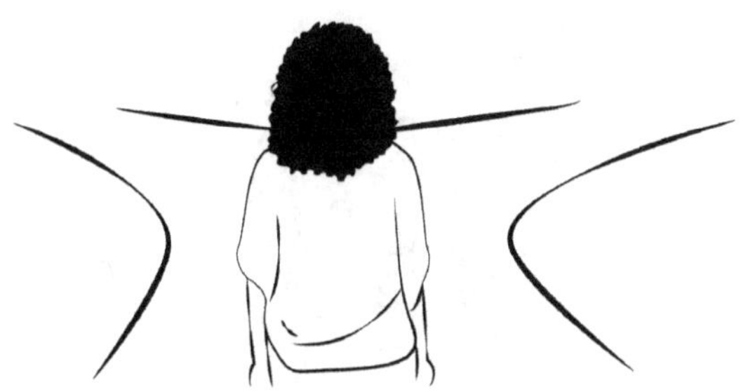

As the evening fades
It's time to play
Through this game we wanted to weigh
As we look at each other play

When you threw the dice and took six steps
ahead
When I passed the bridge which was red
In the game of relationships to see if you'd wait
I knew I would see you there
Waiting to hold my hand in mayday
The street lights were out as I couldn't see you
there
I felt lost in the abyss without a care

Tie and Dye

Tied to the mystery
When I was colourblind in our history
Dyed in a flowery world
But despite life's sorcery
I wrote our memories in a diary
We tied and dyed in each other like a beautiful
scenery

Hot and Cold

You charmed me and I was floored
When we played hot and cold
As I hid behind the pole
You found me in a go
When you hid
And I was hot
You were quick enough to ghost

Silver Lining

Flying over the clouds
Seeing far and wide
All I can see are outlines
A silver light that shines through
Bright as ever
Tell me to keep pushing through
No matter what the situation is
There's hope in all silver linings

Lost and found

We were left disgruntled by the abrupt end
The next three days we couldn't help but vent
This unsettling feeling of wondering what this
meant
This couldn't have been the way we bent
We finally spoke and made amends
Promised to talk about our intent
Before giving our hearts a dent

Games Night

We went out for a games night and beer
With your arms around me like soft fur
You whispered sweet nothings in my ear
At the arcade that was by the pier
We spread the love in the atmosphere
Some moments clear and some a blur
We were filled with joy and a loud cheer

Choices

We always have a choice
Who we want to keep at bay and
Who we want to keep close

We always have a choice
Whether to submit or
Decide the course

We always have a choice
To see the bad and good
For what they are

We always have a choice
To choose what we deserve and
To reject what should be kept afar

Sail Through

Life won't always be rosy
Let's prepare to sail through the rough seas
I'll flow with ease
With no rush and sharp eyes that see
I know how I deserve to feel
Peace and happy at the back of the wheel

Wild Goose Chase

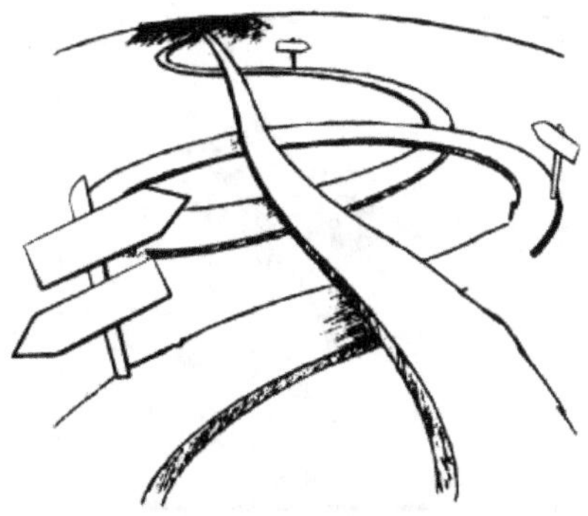

You thought you had set the plot
To chase the one you wanted to lock
But instead saw them flee the spot
Never chase a man, choose grace
Or it becomes a wild goose chase
You'll always get lost in the maze

Swipe Right or Wrong

High hope to find real love
Wrong places to find the above
A few swipes aren't good enough
When you swipe, don't be caught in a cuff
True love takes work and effort in the gulf
In the game of emotions, you'll be rebuffed
This way or that, you decide what's enough
Be wise enough to identify the bluff
Swipe right or left, you build yourself tough

Dating Game

Meeting different people opens up your mind
To the personalities that exist are not one of a
kind
Persistence often blows your mind
To think who is it, you will finally find
After a while monotony hits the grind
You feel like that's it! I am hopelessly blind
Take it as it comes is what settles the mind

Radio

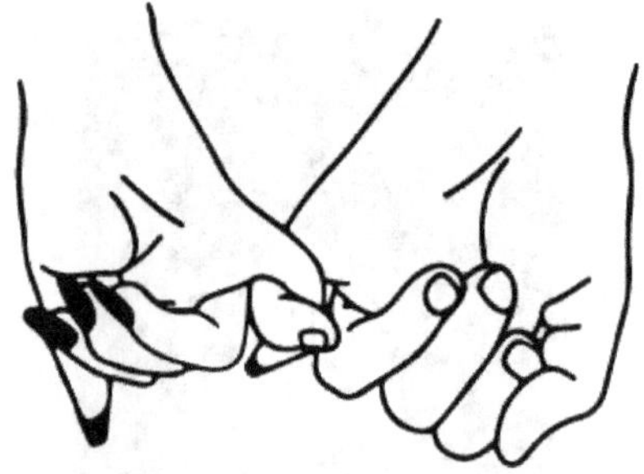

Driving around on country roads
We sang songs playing on the radio
You held my hand as we drove
We discovered our jam early on the road

Green Flag

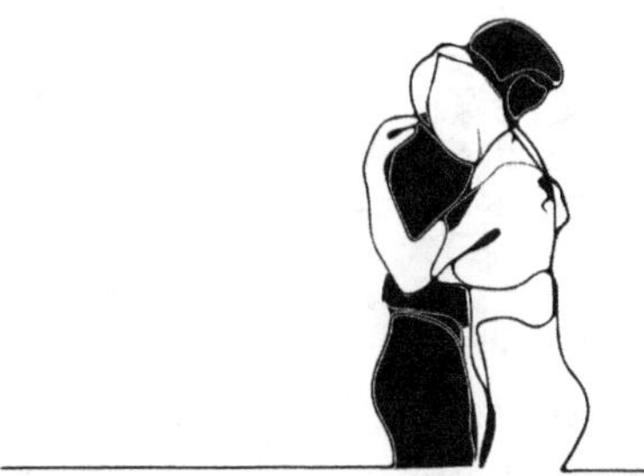

A wish to find a connection
That spreads respect in the roots
Extends trust and understanding to the trunk
The branches full of communication, passion,
and love
The leaves and flowers blossom with happiness
and joy

Music in my Mind

I remember when you sang to me
With a guitar in your hand
As you strummed the strings
Your words played a tune in my heart
As you watched me in the crowd
I was mesmerized as you sang
While I silently screamed with joy in my mind

Stormy Night

The quarrels that we had were like
thunderstorms
Until it poured heavily as I lay on the side
Watching you watch me the entire night
We know the storm hadn't settled just yet
We woke up with a flood of emotions the
following day
Sat with a cup of tea and put our troubles to dry
As the weather cleared so did our minds

Gestures

You admired how my arms move
Noticed my fingers telling a story
My eyes have a language of their own
It's in the body language we find many answers
And the gestures they talk in are a silent
language of their own

Cook Off

A fun day at the farm
We performed a cook-off under the palm
I won two points for being calm
But I lost them to your charm

Turbulence

There are different ways to take someone on a
ride
As most people may take the road
Some may take the boat
It's when you're high in the air
You're delusional and that's unfair
Abort mission due to turbulence should be the
cue
You must come down and be rescued

The right one

When the honeymoon time settles
You peel off the petals
To see the bud for what it nettles
Whether together you feel the mettle
Support each other at all levels
Value each other and revel
It shouldn't ever be about one person performing
the treble
Towards each other you're always gentle

Fight for love

Sitting by the window pane
We watched the dust and the rain
When it settled you took my name
We kept on the game of blame
But realized it didn't help us gain
We remembered our love campaign
Our promise to never go to bed in strain

Heart talk

It's important to be self-aware
As it's important to care
As to how it feels
About being there
It's the feelings you share
That feels, whether it's fair?
To get two people to declare
As you sit across on the chair
Having 'the talk' without the scare

Jammed Door

A knob that wasn't turning
As the lock was jammed
The key was stuck in deep
We kept pulling the door back and forth
Only to realize we used the wrong key